Donald Campbell Nicolson worked as an engineer for several established companies, including a thirteen-year jaunt to sea. When he returned to dry land, he continued working as an engineer, but this time for the Greater Glasgow Health Board. More recently he decided to pursue his love of literature and obtained Twentieth Century Poetry and Drama, supplemented by English urban history.

Following a heart condition and a triple by-pass, his wife insisted it was time to stop work and enjoy a more leisurely lifestyle. He now spends his days writing poetry and short stories.

Child's Song (Sea Time) and Other Poems

Child's Song (Sea Time) and Other Poems

Donald Campbell Nicolson

ATHENA PRESS
LONDON

CHILD'S SONG (SEA TIME) AND OTHER POEMS
Copyright © Donald Campbell Nicolson 2007

ISBN (10-digit): 1 84401 862 8
ISBN (13-digit): 978 1 84401 862 8

First Published 2007 by
ATHENA PRESS
Queen's House, 2 Holly Road
Twickenham TW1 4EG
United Kingdom

Printed for Athena Press

Contents

Memories

Children's Verse

Child's Song (Sea Time)

Sea bells, sea bells, sea bells chime:
Four o'clock, eight o'clock, dinnertime.
Sunrise, sunset, starlight time,
Sea bells, sea bells, sea bells chime.

Middle of the morning, middle of the day,
Sea bells, sea bells, chime away.
Eight bells noon-time, four bells two,
Eight bells four o'clock, watch is through.

Sea bells, sea bells, sea bells chime:
Four o'clock, eight o'clock dinnertime.
Sunrise, sunset, starlight time,
Sea bells, sea bells, sea bells chime.

Holidays

Wee boats, pea boats, boats around the pier
Willie's jumped among the nets
He's in the fishing gear.
He's on his summer holidays
The weather's fine and clear
He's aye about the fishing boats
Down by the pier.

Mother's screaming 'Willie'
And Father's in the pub
And Sister Annie's on the beach,
Eating all the grub.

But Willie's not concerned with that –
The weather's fine and clear –
He's jumped among the fishing nets,
He's in the fishing gear.

Nature

Love Poem

The sea and breeze, the starlight sky,
With all of these in love am I.
The gulls that hover, soar and cry
Above the rigging, in the sky,
Care not for me or for my love
Of leeward breeze and stars above;
But still they follow ship and sail
Through wind and rain, through sleet and hail,
Until the land is gone from sight
And all the sea's agleam with light.

Then do they dive and skim the foam
And rising change their course for home.
The sea and breeze and starlight sky,
With all of these in love am I.

Summertime

Summer's yellow, yellow, yellow,
Yellow, yellow, yellow,
And honey bees with heavy sacs
With humming wings and yellow backs
Fly shimmering past the cornfield stacks
All bright and yellow.

And golden gleams the glistening stream
And fishes golden glitter
In shallow pools with golden banks
When summer's yellow.

Dreams are born on days like these.
The heart beats quicker.
And all things hum and thrum with life:
The round-eared brown gold harvest mice,
The busy ants, the busy bees,
The darting birds among the trees,
And golden hours make up the days
When summer's yellow.

The Catcher

In the hedgerow in summer
Between the dry surface of the loam
And the deep dampness of the last rain
Some little creatures roam.

Blind and silent, black and brown,
They go about their silent tasks
Like anxious soldiers trenching in the field
Fearful of approaching sounds.

Then like some army badly led
They leave the safety of the hedge
And burrow criss-cross through the field
Leaving telltale mounds of dirt as evidence.

Then does the catcher with practised eye
With trident fork and gauntlet hand
Plunge into the summer earth
And some small creature dies.

Stay where you are mankind,
Leave no trail of dirt across your fields.
The catcher waits and watches all of us
And he may be content
To watch mankind destroy his own environment.

Moods

Can I be sad?
There is no point.
Tomorrow joy replaces sadness.
If this was not so,
How could I live?
How could I, below this pale blue sky of spring
With daffodils and small but graceful saxifrages, fail
to sing?

How could I, when all the joy of nature springs to
life,
Refuse to join the happy throng
And add my own enjoyment to this life?
Can I be sad?
There is no point.

Springtime

The day has gone and night, traced with the silver
Finery of the stars, enfolds the sea.
The moon, pale lemon, naked, bright,
With silent stealth applies her magic touch
Across the night.

And lovers, whose eyes reflect the stars, entwine their
arms,
Caress, and hear the sighing sea
That gently strokes the moon-drenched shore
With soothing rhythm.

They kiss and know that this is heaven on earth,
That all the sounds and music of the sea,
The sighs, the endless whisper of the waves
This lovers' symphony, exists for them alone
While all the world's asleep.

But night, the dreaming time moves on.
The stars recede and softly yield to early morning light.
Soft winds disturb the sea, the lovers' sleep
To wake, to love again, to hear the wild birds sing,
For this is spring.

Autumn

Now autumn's come
And summer's barely fled.
The russet leaves, half weight
And summer-dried,
Deep piled, crisp, crackling,
Carpeting the drives,
Drift with the autumn breeze,
And pile in banks, deep gold and brown
Then fly again with wayward gust
Until, rain struck and flooded,
Deep sodden, weighted down,
The gold of summer disappears
And all is autumn brown.

Wintertime

Sometimes it snows at Christmas,
Then everything brightens up.
The weary plodding time from November
With all its bleakness, winds and
Storms are over. There is a new look
To the season, the bleakness is gone.
Christ's spirit fills the air.

Why is this not so from
January to December?
Perhaps we are at fault.
Too many things to do,
Too many things to remember,
Too little time.
But He who knows us well
Forgives our sad forgetfulness
And gives us joy at Christmas time.

Is it true that this is winter?
Why is everything so bright?
Why have snowflakes
Come so beautiful?
Why have snowfalls
Come so bright?

The children know.
They see the life to come.
They have no fear,
For Christ is near.
They know the magic
Of the Christmas story.
The gifts, the parties,
And the joyful time.

But most of all, they know
That Christ was born
On Christmas day,
In wintertime.

The Foxgloves, Thistles and the Heather

Have you seen the summer blooms:
The daises and buddleia?
Or have you watched the moving sea,
The Cirrus clouds and signs of weather?
Or have you seen with artist's eye
The foxgloves, thistles and the heather?

What is it makes the heart beat fast
When August moon shines bright and clear
And soft winds blow and stir the corn
While harvest mice with golden crowns
Climb up the stalks of ripening grain?

How is it that in summer my eye
Is filled with scenes of gleaming gold
Yet all I see when harvest comes
Is stubble, chaff, the scythe and plough
And huge machines that chuff and puff
And blow the grain like golden dust?

Yet far beyond the farmer's fields
In dew-drenched hills with glistening streams
With morning sun and summer weather
The beauty of the Wild remains
In Foxgloves, Thistles and the Heather.

Beauty

Have you seen the heavens all armoured with gold,
With crimson tipped lances like weapons of old,
With orange flags flying, and yellow and green?
It's the Heralds of evening proclaiming their queen.

Have you seen that monarch set Cirrus agleam,
Steep cities in silver and rivers and streams?
Have you seen her retreat (like a moth from flame)
When the sun in the east comes shining again?

Have you felt dew on your feet in the morning,
Felt heat from the sun in the mid afternoon,
Smelled the sweet scent of stock in the evening air,
Felt the spell of a midnight moon?

If you have not then rest awhile
Let beauty step your way,
For all these thing that I write of
Are pleasures of a summer's day.

The Lawn

I watch the golden petals fall
And golden dust spread all around
While daisies, white with golden eyes,
Still carpet all the weed-filled ground.

Then whirling blades with sharpened edge
Cut through the multi-petalled blooms
And leave a swathe of green lawn grass
Where daisies shine like little stars
And buttercups with petals bright
Spread golden dust on daisy pearls.
And as the flowers fade and die
I look upon the green, green lawn
And wonder what I liked the best –
The daisies and the buttercups,
The gold and white of nature's choice,
Or the plain green shroud of cultured lawn.

I know that I shall see again
The daisies and the buttercups,
The golden petals, shining stars,
And I will let them spread and seed
Like precious pearls upon the lawn
Until with golden dust they seem
Like priceless jewels upon the green.

Butterflies

It's magic all around the tree
When butterflies with gossamer wings
Fly shimmering in the noonday sun
And flit from blooms of buddleia
To other plants to gorge and feed
On simple plants like Joe-pye weed.

There are Admirals and Peacocks
And Cabbage Whites and Commas
That decorate the nicest blooms
And a bright kaleidoscope of wings
Of Orange Tips and Speckled Woods
That makes my garden splendid.

How would it be if we couldn't see
What nature does to our bright garden?
Where flowers and weeds and pool side rushes
Contrast with brilliant buddleia bushes,
Where butterflies with brilliant eyes
With gossamer wings and delicate veins,
Add natures gift to my delight
My garden where sweet beauty reigns.

Religion

Hope

A whisper said
'I love you' – so
I turned, I glanced:
Several faces,
No sound.
A glance –
An eyelid flicked –
Was it she?
I cannot say.
Just a whisper,
None to see.
But I feel loved
Because I know
A whisper said
'I love you' – so
I look above,
And then I see
That hope is love
And love is He.

Lesson

In the snow footprints show,
In the sunlight shadows grow,
In the evening stars do gleam,
In the night our minds dream.

In the morning there's a warning,
Ice is on the windowpane.
In our hearts what is the feeling,
Is it sadness, joy, or pain?

If we rise without forgiving
All the faults of yesterday,
There's no sunlight, only shadows,
Shadows darkening all the day.

Don't let darkness win the fight;
Bless your friends and foes alike.
Children rise and be content,
This is what the Lord has sent.

Morning sunlight, winter snow,
Evening starlight, moonshine's glow:
All these things the Lord has sent,
Praise Him all and be content.

Goodbye (Talking to an Angel)

What time is it?
It is time to go.
Time to go where?
It is time to die.
I cannot believe it!
Summer is on the waves,
The seagulls cry,
White horses leap the rocks.
Alive am I,
Loving each moment dawn to dusk;
Hearing the Curlew cry;
Hearing the Wheat-ear in the corn;
Enjoying the late summer's day.
I have nothing to regret
And everything to love
Yet time is gone.
What have I to say?
Quickly! It is time to die.
God is calling.
But there is so much—
Goodbye.

Constant Love

If I love for one moment
Or for spring or summer,
Do I see beyond the barriers
Of this ordinary life?

Do I, in ecstasy, live a life apart?
A momentary, instant life of passion,
Sealed in this loving heart.
A joy concealed from all,
A sanctuary of my own.

If I love for one moment
Or for autumn or winter,
Do I see beyond the barriers
Of this ordinary life?
Or do I live not knowing
The character of the season's change?

No. It's always time for love.
The seasons change, but love
Is constant, unconcerned with passing time.
He who gave us love, gave love Divine.

Voices

Listen, there are voices whispering.
Do you not hear from this stone forest
Whispers of discontent?
Are you not aware of the unsaid words,
The last sighs,
Echoing round these chilly stones?

Do you not hear the mason's chisel
Chip on the granite stone,
Chip away the last character
And, with a final tap,
Seal with a period the epitaph.

Listen, there are voices whispering.
Do you not hear?
No. These sounds are lost on me
For I am coming in.

Question and Answer

Is God crying when it rains?
I don't think so.
Someone said that man's sinfulness
Had brought God low,
But I don't think so.

How could it be that God,
Who made us what we are,
Could shed a tear for every mortal sin
While we believe in Him?

Is this not the problem mankind has?
Not seeing ourselves as mortal beings.
Sinning and believing,
Yet lying and deceiving.

No, God is not crying when it rains,
But he reminds us of the Flood
That we might change our ways
And come to him who shed his blood.

The rain is but a symbol of his care.
It refreshes and cleanses,
It makes us all aware
That he can wash our sins away
With faithfulness and prayer.

Paschal Praise

Long ago we were passed by when angels filled the late
night sky.
How red the lintel and the frame that let the angels know
our name.
The cleansing blood, that saved us then, applies no more –
For Jesus' blood has saved the priest from sacrificial
chores.
No more sacrifice is made that cannot take away our sins,
For by a single sacrifice Christ made perfect those made
holy.
Pilate saw no fault but washed his hands as though to
temper guilt
And passed the choice of sentence to the crowd.
Then was the Lamb of God taken from the stone
pavement for the priests.
He was taken to that place of skulls, crucified, not broken
or destroyed,

But bloodied so that they might look upon the blood of
Him they pierced,
And by this deed the Scriptures were fulfilled; and
everyone deserted Him.

It's in His resurrection that he's seen to conquer all. The
empty grave
Makes bright the lives of all believers – for they are saved.

Promises

I made my promise to you then
And I will make it once again.
There is no need for care or woe
I gave my promise long ago.

Believe me when I say don't fear
And don't forget that I am here,
I long ago took fear away,
I stand by you along the way.

There is no need for sadness now
For I am here to show you how
I gave my life that you might live;
My love did all your sins forgive.

The promise that I made you then won't fade
I love to hear you sing in praise.
You shout the good news to the sky
My birth so man no more shall die.

While praise and prayer both make a gentle sound,
The joyful life and happiness around
And all man's toil is sweet to me.
I gave you this; I set you free.

The things I promised to you then
I promise to you once again,
There is no need for care or woe,
I gave my promise long ago.

The Eternal Song

When I was young I heard a song
And it's been with me all life long.
I've sung and whistled, hummed and dreamed
That melody I heard when young.
I thought it just a melody
That stayed with me throughout my life,
But now I know I heard a song
So beautiful it could not leave,
The notes so clear that every hour
It fills my heart with joy and love.

I heard the song at Christmas time
And I knew then that Christ was here
And I was captive to his song.
Believe me, I have no regrets
My whole life long I've heard the notes,
The joyful tunes, the sacred words,
And I have lived with that sweet song
The Good News that will always be
The message that in later years
Leads into eternity.

Remember Him

Will you remember Him when He is gone?
Will you keep asking how the rock was moved
Or will you simply wonder how the tomb was bare
When every one who saw the violent act knew He was
there?

Will the empty tomb make more impression
Than the words He spoke before Crucifixion?
Or will you fondly think of Him when He was here
And think you should have paid Him some more
attention.

Fear not for you are not alone. Many people ask who
moved the stone.
The mystery deepened when Mary came to see where
He was laid
And an Angel clad in white (so they say) told her that He
was gone
To meet with people in another place to give them
Grace.

Everything He said and promised will come true.

The Angel spoke the truth and filled the tomb with
brilliant light
While He to Galilee made His way to touch the hearts of
those who waited
And let them know the joy and love and hope that He
dispensed is free to all.

Remember Him and what He said
'There is a resurrection of the dead.
All sins can be forgiven and Grace is free,
If you remember me.'

Save Me

I know you made the sky
I know you made the sea
But I'm not sure, dear Lord,
If you made me.

Why am I so imperfect,
If you created me?
Why have I faults so clear
That all can see?

Were you tired or were you sad
That I should turn out quite so bad?
What can I do to change my ways
To change the pattern of my days?

What can I do to ease the pain
That I might just be born again?
Surely there must be a way
To change my life and be set free.

Lord, listen to my prayer I plead
For I don't know another way
To change my life and be set free
From all the sins that trouble me.

Dear Lord, I give you all my life
The life that you have given me.
I give you praise, I give you prayer,
I give you faith, I give you love.

I know that you can set me free.
Dear Lord, my honest prayer must be
SAVE ME.

Every Season Has a Song

Every season has a song
No matter what the weather;
Sometimes the raindrops fastly fall
And sunshine hides its sparkling beams
Behind dark clouds with silver rims.

In spring we hear the birdsong,
In summer time crickets call,
And then we hear the fluttering wings
Of butterflies and birds in flight
And softly whirring bats at night.

Then autumn brings its changes,
The summer colours are gone -
Muted browns and silver glist
And morning frost and autumn cool
Introduce the morning mist.

Then we know that winter's come
And soon the Christ child is born
And we shall hear the happy songs
And Christian voices raised in prayer
That praise our Lord and Saviour.

We'll hear carols, hymns and tunes
That praise the Lord and give hope,
Enrich our lives and let us see
That there is joy and life and cheer,
No matter what the time of year.

The Christmas Boy

When starlight gleams across the sky
And moonbeams spread a yellow light
Across a world that sleeps and dreams
Of miracles and promised joy –
Dependent on an infant boy.
We live in peace and softly pray
That we shall meet when daybreak bright
Dispels the darkness of the night –
The power who promises from above
Forgiveness and eternal love.

Christmas time is such a joy
When infant Christ is brought to mind
And we can see the starlight crown
The moonlight's yellow-gold halo
And remember Him who came to save
The repentant sinners of the world.

Two thousand years have passed since when
A child was born in Bethlehem,
A son whom God had sacrificed
To bear the costs of sinful man

Yet Christ despite his fateful life
Loved man so much he gave his life,
And sent a message after death
To strengthen those who felt bereft:

The Holy Spirit lives today
Praise God and Christ for lasting joy,
Praise Jesus Christ the Christmas boy.

Paradise

If I were invited to attend the City of God at the world's
end
Or scale the heights of Mount Olympus and view the
scenes of great delight in Elysium fields
I'd still remember what God gave the human race
In Adams time, and how we squandered Eden's bliss and
ruined the perfect garden.
And then I'd wonder if I'd sin again and ruin the dream
I'd long envisaged
In my romantic days.
Perhaps I've learned how to be wise and live in God-
ruled Paradise.

There's always hope that I might see Heaven's gates ajar
and beckoning me,
All sins forgiven, and I shall see my advocate who waits
to welcome me.
For Christ welcomes all who turn to him and He, with
arms open wide,
Embraces all who go inside.

Do you believe that Heaven's gate will stay ajar and let
you through
All sins forgiven – where joy is free and lasts through all
Eternity?
Or do you doubt with groans and sighs there's such a
thing as paradise?
Fear not for Christ has promised man to bring him to the
Promised Land.

Remember Him and what He said: 'there is a
resurrection of the dead.
All sins can be forgiven and Grace is free if you
remember me.'

Journey's End

Jesus Christ is my redeemer
He's my saviour and my friend;
I know that He will not leave me
As I reach my journey's end.

Even then I know He'll meet me,
Guide me through the darkest night,
Take me to my Father's mansion,
Give me rest and joyful light.

There's no darkness or black shadows,
No recriminations there;
Only his forgiving presence
Joy and goodness everywhere.

So let us all remember Him
Who forgives us all our sin
Rescues us from all temptations,
Gives us peace and consolation,
As we reach our journey's end.

Jesus Christ is my redeemer –
He's my saviour and my friend;
I know that He will not leave me
As I reach my journey's end.

Love Is Like This

Love is like this – just a sigh and a kiss…
What else is there between heaven and earth?
A vacant space between crops and stars,
Or is there something more that I have missed?
Perhaps I have expected too much,
Perhaps my simple joy has been misplaced.
Maybe there is more to love than a sigh and a kiss.
Yet He who knows us well makes all of us aware
That love, though a sigh and a kiss,
Is heaven's gift to us and a benediction
Of life's eternal quest for love.
And He is waiting for our prayers of love.
Please sigh and think of Him
Who was betrayed by a kiss,
And how our lives were changed by this betrayal.
We know that even after the foul act
(The Judas kiss that sealed his fate)
He left to humankind the knowledge
That love is like this – just a sigh
And a kiss that changes the world.

Christmas Tree Angel

Raise me up that I might see
The angel on the Christmas tree.
There's fairies and there's elves
And flightless birds and baubles.
There's sparkling globes and tinkling bells
And lanterns brightly glowing,
But overall the angel rules
And spreads a Christian blessing.
Goodwill is spread with love and joy
With equal shares to everyone,
And we remember Christ today
And all the work that He has done
And we with joyful hearts will pray
For Christ who gave us Christmas day.

Praise

Now summer's lease has near expired
And autumn's gold is promised,
And Christian hearts with joy are fired
While starlit nights reveal to all
The beauty of the evening sky
And God's eternal presence.

Praise Him who gave us sun and stars,
Who gave us seasons – joy and life.
Who gave us all the things we need:
The crops, the grain, the food we eat;
And in our greatest times of need
Is counsellor guide and saviour.

Praise Him whose son died for our sins
And promised us redemption,
Praise Jesus Christ the advocate
Who speaks for all repentants,
Who is our hope, our joy, our life
And promises us eternal life.

Amen.

Memories

Sea Time

There's a squeak and a squeal as eight bells peal
And a rattle on the for'ard deck.
And the ship gives a roll as the helmsmen change
But it's soon brought into check.

There's cocoa in the chart house, sweet and strong,
And a small blue light by the door.
There's a binnacle light and a radar light –
In the sky there's a million more.

There's a rustle of charts and the tick of a clock
And the sextant's out of its case.
Then the mate's on the bridge and he takes his sights
And the lookout takes his place.

And all watch long there's the sound of a song
In the slapping of waves on deck,
And the stars are bright in the dark clear night.
And the log keeps its nautical check.

There's a squeak and a squeal as eight bells peal
And the watch is passed away,
And the look-out climbs from his island perch
In the crisp clear light of day.

Dream

Listen to me.
Time is flying past.
Hang on to that sweet dream,
You know the one,
The dream you cannot tell to anyone
Because by telling you destroy
The image and the joy.

You may suffer sadness
By telling all to those
Who live in discontent.
For in your dreams there's joy and life
And when you sacrifice
Your own sweet dream
To those sad people
Wasting their lives away
You sacrifice yourself.

The image goes
And you are left a dream amiss.
Listen to me.
Time is flying.
Hang on to that sweet dream,
For there encased
Tomorrow's joy exists.

Homesick

Oh well, I mind how we played upon the mountain side
as youths,
With neither care nor sorrow nor woeful glance to hide,
And well, I mind the bright sunset on West Loch
Tarbert's shore
And happy evenings talking in days of yore.

And how I mind the fishing, and the climbing and the
fanks,[1]
And all the fine young friends I had and all our boyish
pranks,
And how I mind the smell of peat, of bannocks[2] and of
brose[3]
And the lamplight in the evening as the pale moon rose.

---

[1] A place where crofters gather their sheep for sheering or dipping; a sheep pen.
[2] Thick, round flat oatcakes baked on a griddle.
[3] Ground green peas mixed with water to as a soup, sometimes with fat added, to
be eaten as a soup.

I mind the road to Scalpay and the road to Rodil too,
Those winding miles of beauty and the East Loch
brightly blue;
I mind the road to westward and the Clisham's misty
heights,
And the whispering of the ocean in the clear still nights.

But best of all I mind the folk, their lilting highland
tongue,
Their kindness and their laughter and their art of staying
young;
And when I cross the oceans and sail across the seas
My heart is always crying for the outer Hebrides.

Yesterday's Joy

I've seen dark clouds go scudding by
No joy within the evening sky.
No moon, no light, no stars to sight,
A rising sea and a wind that bites.

I've seen the rising sea surmount
The fo'c's'le head and all about,
Then rushing, slushing, find its way
Through flooded scuppers and away.

And when the storm has passed me by
I've watched the beauty of the sky
And seen the masthead's yellow light
Waltz between stars, silver bright.

But now, retired, I sit and see
Within my mind my time at sea,
Reliving life from man to boy
Recapturing yesterday's joy.

Homeward Bound

Fair highland hills that beckon me,
To you I'll soon return.
I'm tired of wandering o'er the sea,
I'm tired of tropic sun.

I long to see the glistening streams,
The heather on the hill,
To watch the sunset on the loch
When all is quiet and still.

I long to hear the seagull's cry,
To watch them wheel and glide on high,
To light the lamp when day is done
And live at peace with everyone.

I long to see my own folk,
To see their kindly smiles,
I wish to spend my last days
Far in the Western Isles.

The Retirement

Time flies past and all our yesterdays
Are but an instant.
Who is this old servant?
This trusted officer of men,
This colleague whose time is spent
And whose achievements we admire?
Who is this happy man,
This happy man we praise
For kindness
And for his considered ways?

Is he the boy who
One instant past stood up to cheer
And by the time the last
Echoing shout had died
Found he was a man,
And in this reality sighed,
And by the time his breath exhaled
Found his colleagues wishing him well
In his new leisure days
Found them pressing praise and
With each well constructed compliment
Advanced the termination of his working days?

Who is this old servant?
He is the boy who long ago
Stood on the yellow sand
And turned around a little at a time
Eyes shuttered tight – for an instant blind –
Then opened them again to gaze upon,
With each alternate step and blink, a new horizon.

Goodbye, dear friend – you have turned again –
You have blinked –
Your world is all anew.
We are your yesterdays,
Step out across the sand to new enchantments.
We wish you well – keep turning round
For time flies past and all our yesterdays are but an
instant.

The Dancing Years

When I was young I always danced
But kept my dancing feet upon the ground.
It wasn't my career that made me dance,
Just a joyful feeling of exuberance.

I loved each moment when I danced around,
Had thoughts of Fred Astaire and danced with a joy
That kept me dancing all the time
And filled my leisure hours when I was a boy.

But even though my years advanced
I danced and danced and still believed
That joy and love would always be
The dance to dance through all my life
Into Eternity.

Memories

Sandalwood, sandalwood, scent of the east,
Frankincense, rosemary, sweet scented briar,.
All of the scents that remind me of you
Come sweet and soft on the evenings cool breeze
And linger and last me the whole night through
Until in the morning in dawn's soft light
The scents of the east are faded and gone.

But though I remember it's not the same
As being together; enjoying the sweet pleasure
Of long summer days and moments of rapture
That filled the days with joy and with laughter;
But I must settle for things as they are
And look to evening and dreams of caresses
The memory of you and loves sweet embraces.

When memory fades and young thoughts are gone,
And winter has come and sunbeams are low,
There's still a consciousness stirring within,
A heart that's slow and a sight that is dim.
My heart beats quicker and memories are fresh
And scents remind me of times that are past
When the heart wasn't slow and I was young.

Sandalwood, sandalwood, scent of the east,
Frankincense, rosemary, sweet scented briar.
These scents remain though the heart is now slow
And eyes that are dim can see little now,
I remember you well while the scents linger on
Until in the morning they faded and are gone.

Night Watch

When evening stars peep out and smile upon the sea
And homing gulls give out their melancholy cries,
I feel alone in this huge bowl of midnight blue,
Alone with God, the sea, and the wide, wide sky.

My colleagues sleep, or play, or watch the engines whirl,
Not far removed from me, yet many worlds away,
Perhaps they talk of times ashore, or dream of friends,
Or tend machines to while the long night's watch away.

But I look out and face the blanket of the night
A counterpane of stars spread out above my head
And I ring out the bells and cry the lights,
A solitary watchman of the night.

Homeland

I dream of the highlands and heather-clad islands
When I am straying so far, far, away
And then for my homeland I sigh with deep longing,
I sigh for the sight of my sweet Castlebay.

When I was young I set off for the city –
I went to Glasgow seeking fortune and fame,
I joined a tramp steamer and sailed for the Indies
And I've never seen my sweet homeland again.

There's nights I lie dreaming and hear cattle lowing
And dream that I'm going to Castlebay pier,
And then I awaken, my dreams are forgotten;
I find myself back in the warm tropic air.

I'm just an old seaman that's lost all his money,
That's wasted his life and has sold all his gear;
I'm too old for sailing and soon I'll be passing,
I cannot help sighing for things I hold dear.

I dream of the highlands and heather-clad islands
When I am straying so far, far away
And then for my homeland I sigh with deep longing,
I sigh for the sight of my sweet Castlebay.

Past Times

Sometimes I think of times gone by
And memories fill my days,
Some good, some bad, some very sad,
Some magical, some sparkling,
Some dark or very grey;
But always there's a star that shines,
A sun that brightens day,
And in my mind there is a song
That chases clouds away:
Jesus Christ is my redeemer,
He dispels the darkest thoughts,
He brightens dreams and sweetly brings,
A memory of brighter things,
Of love, of joy, of happy days,
A time of songs and hymns of praise.
And I can face my memories,
That trouble me and make me sad.

For Christ will always be to me
A joyous friend who takes my hand
To guide me to the Promised Land
Where all clouds have a silver lining,
And darkest night is bright with stars
A canopy of hope and dreams,
Of memories that let me see
That Christ is love and he loves me.

When Summer's Roses Petals Fall

When summer's roses petals fall
And summer's blush has faded,
When ardent thoughts cool with the breeze
Autumn comes and love is spent,
We'll still remember times of joy
When roses bloomed before the fall.

When love, lacks lustre, dulls and dims
And autumn's shadows lengthen
And snowflakes dust the evergreens
As winter time approaches,
We brighten up and love's reborn
With joy and cheer at Christmas.

How beautiful is Christmas time
With reborn love and passion,
With hearts abrim with joy and hope
We know that love does not die,
But simply rests and waits for Him
Who loves us in all seasons.

And we know well when spring comes round,
And seedlings shoot and spring flowers bloom,
That love like joy and summer bliss
Will come again when roses blush.

www.ingramcontent.com/pod-product-compliance
Lightning Source LLC
Chambersburg PA
CBHW031148250726
48655CB00002B/885